Beautiful Birds

PARROTS

By Kristen Rajczak Nelson

Gareth Stevens
PUBLISHING

Please visit our website, www.garethstevens.com. For a free color catalog of all our high-quality books, call toll free 1-800-542-2595 or fax 1-877-542-2596.

Library of Congress Cataloging-in-Publication Data

Names: Rajczak Nelson, Kristen, author.
Title: Parrots / by Kristen Rajczak Nelson.
Description: New York : Gareth Stevens Publishing, [2023] | Series: Beautiful birds | Includes index.
Identifiers: LCCN 2021035980 (print) | LCCN 2021035981 (ebook) | ISBN 9781538275207 (set) | ISBN 9781538275214 (library binding) | ISBN 9781538275191 (paperback) | ISBN 9781538275221 (ebook)
Subjects: LCSH: Parrots–Juvenile literature.
Classification: LCC QL696.P7 R35 2023 (print) | LCC QL696.P7 (ebook) | DDC 598.7/1–dc23
LC record available at https://lccn.loc.gov/2021035980
LC ebook record available at https://lccn.loc.gov/2021035981

First Edition

Published in 2023 by
Gareth Stevens Publishing
29 East 21st Street
New York, NY 10010

Editor: Kristen Nelson
Designer: Andrea Davison-Bartolotta

Photo credits: Cover Ondrej Prosicky/Shutterstock.com; p. 1 Napachara Tochaona/Shutterstock.com; p. 5 Cavan-Images/Shutterstock.com; pp. 7, 24 (toes) Gleb Aitov/Shutterstock.com; p. 9 (top right) Zeehan Ahmed/Shutterstock.com; p. 9 (top left) Donatas Dabravolskas/Shutterstock.com; p. 9 (bottom right) Bappa Pabitra/Shutterstock.com; p. 9 (bottom left) Gabriela Beres/Shutterstock.com; p. 11 Alan Jeffery/Shutterstock.com; pp. 13, 24 (rain forest) Fireflycreative/Shutterstock.com; p. 15 Reto Buhler/Shutterstock.com; p. 17 narikan/Shutterstock.com; pp. 19, 24 (beak) Natalia Johnson/Shutterstock.com; p. 21 Valerija Polakovska/Shutterstock.com; p. 23 Kurit afshen/Shutterstock.com.

Printed in the United States of America

Contents

Parrots are birds.
They can be green.
They can be red
or blue.

They have curved beaks
They have four toes.

There are more than 300 kinds.

Macaws are some of the largest.

They live in all over
the world.
They like rain forests.

They eat nuts
and seeds.
They eat fruit.

They are kept as pets.
They live at zoos too.

They are smart birds. Some can copy speech.

They live a long time.
Some live 80 years!

They are pretty birds!

Words to Know

beak rain forest toes

Index